Dogma

poems by

Nancy Devine

Finishing Line Press
Georgetown, Kentucky

Dogma

Copyright © 2019 by Nancy Devine
ISBN 978-1-63534-917-7 First Edition
All rights reserved under International and Pan-American Copyright Conventions. No part of this book may be reproduced in any manner whatsoever without written permission from the publisher, except in the case of brief quotations embodied in critical articles and reviews.

ACKNOWLEDGMENTS

Publisher: Leah Maines

Editor: Christen Kincaid

Cover Art: https://creativecommons.org/publicdomain/zero/1.0/deed.en

Author Photo: Chuck Devine

Cover Design: Nancy Devine

Printed in the USA on acid-free paper.
Order online: www.finishinglinepress.com
also available on amazon.com

Author inquiries and mail orders:
Finishing Line Press
P. O. Box 1626
Georgetown, Kentucky 40324
U. S. A.

*Dogma is for the glorious creatures that bring joy,
as well as challenge, to our lives.
"...the potent presence and consolation of the animal body..."*

from Mark Doty's Heaven's Coast

1

For nearly three weeks I've watched,
waited; tonight I go to him,
a shy lab at the edge of my yard;
the distance between us,
mere breath, a fence,
thin like branches of a young ironwood,
quiet, like the tree itself,
shouldering late summer along its barbed boughs.

He is a hunger I've never seen,
though it devours me daily
in long swallows I can't climb.
But I hold out my hand.
And he starts to nuzzle it
but then remembers that fence,
electrified now with our desires
for one another as if we want to
found a new planet
or christen a boat that
has floated near the dock we share.

(Other creatures do have their water—
the sap that runs from a birch wood
before it rots on its feet
as the trunk thickens at the middle and then falls,
a slip)

This lab and I don't know what
we have in this silent heat,
although it could be this fence.
I close my eyes and step through the gate,
the latch easier to undo than I expected
and so am I.

2

The lab, he sleeps in a spray
of sunlight that comes in
through the front picture window,
and when he shuns his dish,
I hand-feed him bits of bread,
pieces of meat I sequester
at the edge of my own plate.

I expected him to be gentle,
but these meals are serene;
the hours relent and stop begging for more.
Before I sleep
I no longer imagine the next day as a guillotine,
chopping off tomorrow's empty head.
I tilt my hips toward the bed,
lengthen, as if my spine
is the baculum of night
and something new will be.

3

But then the sky posts its advertisement
and suddenly a pregnant collie curls
at the cold corrugated metal
of an egress window at my house.
She'll be timid when I approach,
I say, as I drink coffee insipid
as March. But, when I drag my feet through
the new snow, she lifts her heads, wags
all she can.
My left hand's gentle gesture her signal,
she comes in,

where she takes to an old pillow
I've left out, although my shepherd mix
died two winters ago.
And we know how winters go,
furious then calm then angry,
mercurial as my lost mother raging now on some distant
sea or plain.

In a week, the collie gives birth in blankets
at the foot of my bed;
when the pups mewl like the dead,
I know I can never let them go.
I find new contentment in a different sleep
I tender.
I dream the gods close and each one takes my hand.

4

Another? she asks, her brow furrowed,
a stave but no music.
Yes. Not a problem.
For a week until I find a new apartment
he pleads, his bags
a Stonehenge of fleeing around his feet.
Certainly, the seven days become
a fortnight that gives birth to months,
new times bounded by bark.
An epiphany of *certainly*,
a litany of *absolutely no problem,*
a tentacle of *sure* and *you bet*
and *I can do that for a while.*

I've lost track of keeping track
without beads to count
pushed by mouths to feed,
then that clean-up.
Cell's long division
momentarily unchecked.
You can't worry about yourself
anymore…that's how I like it,
among others.

5

So the square-faced poodle's
part rottweiler and will protect me
when I no longer have a gun.
Its pups, the same,
though their eyes have barely opened
in each of their heads,
small and valuable coin purses
who hold all I treasure.
Such soft small creatures
I cradle in the bowl of my hand
they try to suckle my fingers.
How can any of this be wrong?

It's easy to be careful when you come in
the front door; watch your step is what
we all do every day.
Step. Watch. Even
if it's too easy to look elsewhere
as I have often practiced.
Oh, where have they been?

6

I remember the broken floor boards,
the sofa stripped to springs and slats,
the kitchen up-turned
as if each glass and cup
could be filled with the floor.

There was plastic across the backdoor,
wind badgered it—
the sound—boys boxing
sheets of metal instead of attending school.
Some slush in the bath tub drain,
a thin stream from the faucet,
nearly spittle when I wanted to get clean.

One day, everyone walked outside
for a long time, and I was left behind
in the ghost-less house of my upbringing.
When they returned, no hello's.
What I said is immaterial, though not transcendent.
What I thought is
"I am not back" as I faced
them, slouched a bit,
some weak hand on my shoulder.

7

My brow bone,
when we are face to face,
comes just above hers—the collie's.
My eye resides there:
ball to socket,
hand over fist.
A willing survival of the fittest
or a broken vase glued back together.

A transmission model:
thoughts passing from me to
her....or I'm the great Kreskin
versed in canine,
the echolalia of scattered ancestors.

Not at all.
Rather a wholeness:
the tower of Babel
turned upside down and inside out,
so that every language has a chance,
is put in the ground,
all become seeds which grow together
so that everyone understands everyone...
Man and woman, bird and kite,
bark and, obviously, no-bite.

8

Ask Hitler
how one becomes too many.
He'd know about four then 40,
the geometric progression
of it, the ecstasy of exponents.
But ah....this is different,
so different.
Small mouths make ladles
of their tongues and drink what pours from me.
They are congregations of looking up,
reverence in the morning when the day ahead
is a toxic gruel you try not to spoon from.

So don't ask Hitler
how anything works...not the buses
whose backs seep invisible poison, that serpentine
the air with malice;
the grocery attendants, vicars who sneer
and cajole on the manager's behalf
while he dusts his desk with his mistress's
unmentionables.
I am loved. That is all. All.

9

Car lights a rushed strobe
through my late night window,
a tear of brakes, their pads shredded...
the dismal disco of daylight's end.
But when I go to look, nothing,
save a blue-black shadow
in the vapors of dark that covet any morning
brave enough to approach.

Familiar, tail curled like a cord
from a vacuum, shoulders lowered,
the jowl slack as a skein of used yarn.
This one, too, shall be mine I say
as the shadow turns and walks toward me
from the road,
finds the porch and we all know that the porch
is the first step into any house....a woman's,
a child's, an empress's, a dungeon.
I've made a palace, I know.
Tails travel its lengths every day.
I've quit sweeping the night with loss
and throw it away.

10

Floral. The smell is floral
like the perfume bottle
on my grandmother's chest of drawers,
that jeweled atomizer:
the ball to spray and only air comes out
though the smell
is still there and it's floral,
what late afternoon's warm breeze
lifts and presents at my windows' mullions.

The collie's ears carry this,
pungent but beautiful,
like too much peony
from the fuchsia petals
or the roses drying on their screens
in the garage.

When I pull the collie in, I nuzzle her
because I want to be drunk on that aroma,
a shade less than fetid,
much before horrible.
Floral. The smell really is floral
and it almost has that taste...

11

This spring I'll hire him or some brother
to come over and clean up
with his Bobcat.
He can push it all way behind the house
where it can dry in the sun come summer,
become white
as the chalk our father's augur used to hit
when he worked,
dug holes in our fields for apple trees and cherry bushes.

The white can wish itself into a powder,
the dogs' waste a fine talc,
a final and
benign dust that's gone by fall.
And in spring again,
I'll plant more climbing roses there,
William Baffin, John Cabot,
who'll yearn toward Canada,
prickling our border.

My brother's good with the bucket,
can finesse it,
make the spot
flat as the prairie around us,
the one that is wont to swallow us
as if we are just soup…that one
with the severest need to drink.

12

No dreams remain in the morning.
Not even wisps of memory or a certain
settling in my shoulders. Nothing.
So I do not waste my wakefulness.

I watch, sometimes, the cinema of sleep
of one of the dogs—the first lab
or a collie puppy.
The legs employed in some hell-for-leather
run along an open field,
eyes fluttering, following the action
of a rabbit pulled out of the magic hat
that's REM sleep,
the paws flipping up and down,
levers against the late spring ground,
the thaw finished,
solstice sipping her tea near the moon.

13

A car circles four times. A carrion, a vulture,
an Ascaris worm considering its feasts
that you'll curl around a small stick on your arm
until it breaks. I avoid the window; instead I rely on a shadow
cast those four times on the wall I painted
the color of new butter. You'd swear it's soft and
pliable, fondant in your hands and sweet.

At first, the absence of shadow worries me.
The driver could be off finding another.
But the emptiness's old comfort returns
and I swaddle two of the collie pups
in the crescents of my arms,
the crooks where love should live
and is not stolen,
where favor should begin as effortlessly
as an hour.

The day slips away quietly; tomorrow
returns with its cold companion: the quiet.

14

The lady who came from the car
says that I wish I were power.
She believes that I've too much
to care for with my too-little.
She twirls the words "hate" and "cruel"
in her mouth with a joy I've not seen
since the pregnant collie bounded toward me
and let me be her tallest surrogate.

"We'll need to take away" and "some so sick"
and I insist the dogs will be afraid,
that they are connoisseurs of freedom
and only what I can give,
their palettes never weaned
from the drink of me,
the wash up of my legs.

She's rude and asks me what that is:
I fetch the notes of "love" and "tenderness"
from the corners of my thinking where I've put
such stuff. This is my bark. It is.
When she doesn't seem to hear me,
I say, "I'm the leader," which I'd not realized
before. "The Alpha," I say. The Omega, too, I think.
But the trucks arrive and begin
to take just everything as if it's...
packed.

15

She says the smell is
foul, fetid, fecal.
*C'mon. which
f is up? Fecund?*
How could I stand it? Unbearable, right?
So feral?
Something other rides the air
like a cape or kite.
Fey?
It's not what she thinks,
nosy woman
coming in to flout
what I have.

I know the good done here
and I am equal to the task:
faithful, forthright,
the cleaning up, the mopping,
tending, taking care
as someone should have done for me.
Forlorn, frightened.

The only stench....when people
do not and oh how they do.
Fickle?
It's all so *frightening*,
as in *f you*.
You're no more than an effigy.

16

There's not a yellow school bus in the yard
that holds 50 dying dogs,
mange on the seats,
slick along the steering column,
no stench that crowds oxygen from the air.
None of that. ...tautology of tails.
The terminal distant, not even imagined.
What I have not yet done, I will do...
feed and water, watch the withers with my hands.
Not pet to have but to do...
Isn't that why we brought dogs in to the fire with us
not just so they could feel its warmth
but so we could feel its warmth along
the rippling muscles of the backs
or the jowls,
not the reflection of heat and flame,
but that heat and flame of us purposeful
needed by the animals we keep?

17

They're carried out like jail-birds,
protesters, trying to twists
from hands, gyves that won't relent.
Howls careen
from house to truck or van.
I'm not allowed to help,
must wait in the kitchen
at the table with the woman
who says it will be better
as she stares at my brow
as if I'm beyond beaten.
She's younger than me,
her face and hands supple,
her mouth a food-slit,
a talk dispenser,
a lie chute,
an incubator of wrong done to me
now. As the collie's cries
squat in my ears,
lay claim to all I consider,
more taken away:
the soot scraped from the chimney,
ashes to be commingled with dirt,
fires gone as if all we had was water
and this indelible want.

18

Tonight, I'm alone in the house.
The dogs taken,
just me, mostly taken, too,
though I've some, enough, I guess.
The TV's broken, the refrigerator's
got an unsteady grind to it, a re-charging
that makes no sense. Is it the Freon going bad
or breaking loose?
Two cookie sheets on the stove.
Someone's canted the cereal box
so it leans on the cookie jar. The buttermilk
carton the only green around, and
a can of peaches could be opened
with a church key, the most inaccurately named
tool there is—not a heavy wooden door or steeple
for miles. Nothing at all to chase.
Nor a tail.

19

No one has ever said these words to me:
roll over and play dead.
Unneeded.
Every person's face is an instruction manual
on how to read him or her.
The flourish of a hand. Stop.
Just stop.
They think I'm some stack
of blank pages
where they can write
what they long ago copied
from a lecture or a textbook.
I used to think they'd erase it all
beyond smudge.
I could never have imagined this:
how they annotate and
rip sheets from me
until I'm barely the spine
that holds it together,
all that data collected for some tome.
(Or would it be tomb?)

20

Everyone has been here.
All have cleaned and sorted
and re-ordered and mopped
and tackled and heaved
and admonished and warned
and instructed and assured.
I've been agreeable
and then docile and
submissive, contrite, if you will;
my home and I are rehabilitated.
I understand this.
Someone will do and I will be...
this is the agreement we reach.
Dog days, dog tired, dog-gone—
all gone.
But you must believe this:
that whimpering, a yowling
that rises at the edge of my property
behind the garage
beneath a cottonwood older than I am
will not go unheeded;
if it truly were a sleeping dog,
I would never let it lie,
but I would.

21

Do the dogs know I have abandoned them?
They're to be scattered among new homes
and owners like grass seed cupped in the hand
and spread carelessly, as if all we had
were stalks to stab and squander?
Do they know that I am sorry,
so I collect what's left....
my expired driver's license,
which is, in no way, a mirror,
an address book,
a newspaper article about us,
a hoard of lies that should be tossed in the trash?
These fit easily into a small brown bag that closes with snow crunch
in the cinch of my gloved grip.
A shovel fits easily into my hand,
claw around bone,
then its spade into the ground at the property's edge
where I dig and dig until it's too dark to distinguish
dirt from sky, sky from moan, me from moan.
It all goes in,
this makeshift, last minute votive of me-
the worry, the dread,
the bones of my being,
the marrow sucked from them by
the drone of the steady mouth of that woman,
gone with the rest of them,
tucked into hideous lights' alcoves.
I'm now covered, concentrated, soiled.
Do the stars anymore have the energy of listen?
Do I remember the effort of want?

22

But I have a dream. It swoops
into the bottom of my sleep,
rests its talons, for a moment,
on my knowing,
where it has been so long
since something's perched.
Flames, full, the orange and blue
flowering from my house,
soot, a dark pollen where no bees light.
It's the dogs barking outside
that brings the firemen
who stand around wishing
the conflagration out,
their wills becoming water.
The burning goes, and when the men take the dogs
into their arms, bodies
fuse as if soldered.
Then singing, petals,
a cache of melody revealed
as birds find the nearby trees,
build with the suddenly cooled remains
nests from which nothing is ever taken,
pendants of fur, grass braided into a home.
When I look at my arms,
I swear I see the inklings of pin feathers,
hear wind's flourish in my hollow bones
that makes song,
and then, like a sudden explosion,
I wake up. Because waking is mostly up and up...

Thank you

I owe an ongoing thank you to Lurlynn Franklin who encouraged me to send me work out for publication.

I must also thank Pam Fisher for listening to and supporting me; our rescue collie Apple for letting me kiss her snout; my trivia team for continuing to hang out with me even though they've come to know me quite well; Bridget Ryberg for her unbelievable energy and generosity; Laura Wendt for being steadfast; Kim, Rhiannon and Jessica for not only writing blurbs for my work but also for their talent and willingness to share them; my parents for so much; and my husband for his love and capacity.

Nancy Devine, a three-time Pushcart Prize nominee, is a writer, whose poetry, short fiction and essays have appeared in a number of online and print literary magazines and journals, including *Bellevue Literary Review, Midwestern Gothic-A Literary Journal, Stirring-A Literary Collection, Berfois* and *Referential Magazine*. Her chapbook of poems, *The Dreamed*, was published by Finishing Line Press in 2016.

Devine, originally from Minot, North Dakota, recently retired from teaching high school English in Grand Forks, North Dakota, where she lives. She did her undergraduate work at the University of North Dakota, Grand Forks, and Minot State University. In 1997, she received Master of Science from UND. She lives in Grand Forks with her husband and their rescue collie.

www.ingramcontent.com/pod-product-compliance
Lightning Source LLC
LaVergne TN
LVHW041522070426
835507LV00012B/1745